The House of the Octopus

THE OCTOPUS

THE
HOUSE
OF THE
OCTOPUS

ESSAYS ON THE REAL-LIFE
"CTHULHU CULT" OF THE PACIFIC

EDITED BY
JASON COLAVITO

ALBANY, NEW YORK
JASONCOLAVITO.COM
2012

Published by Jason Colavito, Albany, New York

This book has been typeset in Charis SIL

ISBN: 978-1-105-95794-9

www.JasonColavito.com

CONTENTS

INTRODUCTION

JASON COLAVITO

I N "The Call of Cthulhu" (1926), H. P. Lovecraft described a global cult that worshiped the octopus-headed extra-terrestrial god Cthulhu, his minions, and the megalithic undersea city in the Pacific where they rested dead but dreaming until the day of Cthulhu's glorious resurrection:

> There had been aeons when other Things ruled on the earth, and They had had great cities. Remains of Them [...] were still to be found as Cyclopean stones on islands in the Pacific. They all died vast epochs of time before men came, but there were arts which could revive Them when the stars had come round again to the right positions in the cycle of eternity.

While Lovecraft's undersea monster drew on a number of mythic sources, surprisingly and unbeknownst to Lovecraft, there was a real religion in the Pacific that reproduced with uncanny accuracy the major details of the Cthulhu myth as given in the story.

One of the most intriguing of Pacific deities was the Sa-moan god Fe'e (equivalent to the Tongan god called Feke or

Tutula), the god of violence, who lived in a stone palace under the sea and had the form of a giant octopus. This god also had a megalithic stone temple in Samoa, and it was thought that he incarnated as an octopus. When these incarnations died, they were buried in his temple to be reborn in his undersea palace. The Fe'e's megalithic temple at Samoa was called *Fale o le Fe'e*, the "House of the Octopus," and in Lovecraft's day it was believed to be the fabulously ancient work of a lost civilization, though today we know it is only a few centuries old. Just as Cthulhu was said to bring madness to his followers, the followers of Fe'e prayed to him for the blinding madness of red rage.

The following essays report the legend of the Fe'e through the eyes of the British consul in Samoa, William B. Churchward, and the scholar-missionaries George Turner, John B. Stair, and E. E. V. Collocot.

What you are about to read seems like something straight out of Lovecraft. But it is all true.

1 IN SEARCH OF THE "HOUSE OF THE OCTOPUS"[1]

WILLIAM B. CHURCHWARD

THIS morning I put into execution an intention I had had in mind for many a long day, and, accompanied by the Judge and M., started on a pilgrimage in search of the 'Fale o le fe'e,' or, in English, 'the house of the octopus,' which in Samoa, as in many other Pacific Islands, is the personification of the devil; and a very appropriate one too, for a more hideous-looking monster than a large octopus, with its repulsive colour and loathsome slimy arms, threateningly waving and curling as if in dire torture, seeking to grasp their prey, does not exist. However, in spite of its appearance and the exalted position it has been given as chief evil spirit, the Samoans convert the octopus into a favourite article of food, and reverse the proceedings his Satanic Majesty is generally given credit for, by devouring him instead of his devouring them.

---

[1] Excerpted from William B. Churchward, *My Consulate in Samoa* (London: Richard Bentley and Son, 1887).

Starting from Apia about ten o'clock, with two natives to carry our food and a change of clothes, we crossed the 'Vaisigago' about a mile from Apia, and walking up the bank of the river, on the outskirts of the 'Vaivasa' plantation, we soon came to the bush village of 'Magiagi.' Here we picked up a third native, and dividing the load equally between the three, plunged into the narrow track, made almost impassable by a strong undergrowth of pineapples, leading through a very lovely tropical forest.

It was the same old Samoan bush, resplendent with bright-coloured flowers, and fantastically wonderful in its glorious leafage, sympathetically sheltering us from the sun's now brazen rays. Beyond a few bi ids of no remarkable appearance or size, this bush was devoid of animal life; but, to our cost, we found that it was by no means so with regard to insects—the bloodthirsty mosquitoes, the worst I ever experienced, reminding us of their proximity on every occasion of a halt. We were kept so much employed with these annoying creatures that for miles we thought of nothing else, and speculated considerably as to what on earth could be the use for them, and what they live upon when they can't find a human victim. To all appearance, and most decidedly to our experience, human blood seemed to be their natural diet; but then what do the other thousand billions of the beasts do who never see or taste it? It struck us that Nature had not dealt quite fairly with this bird of prey, as here he was almost big enough to be termed, in raising him in places where, but for the godsend of idiotic Britishers—who will penetrate everywhere, no matter in what discomfort or for what useful purpose—the unfortunate insect would have to put up with sucking trees and stones.

On the way, for about two miles, we found occasional clumps of cocoa-nuts, bread-fruit, and oranges, but these soon ceased; whilst every now and then we would pass through spaces which bore signs of long-past occupation.

Plodding slowly on through the many and varied timber trees—from the ready-made-board tree, with its irregular wide-spreading buttresses, to the 'musu-oe,' standing erect with a mathematical perpendicularity, as regular as if its trunk had been turned out of some workshop, surmounted with its crown of splendid foliage, whose flower produces the most valued scent and head ornament for the Samoans—and gaining height at every step, we came suddenly upon a sight worth looking at. It was an enormous banyan tree, whose branches, hung with many varieties of bush-ferns, supported flowery parasites of all descriptions, festooned with hanging mosses and lovely creepers. It rose to a great height above its tallest bush companions, its aërial roots descending in a vast twisted network, about eighty feet in depth, and covering a yearly increasing expanse of ground to the effacement of its neighbours. It is, I believe, of the same species as the Indian tree, and its phenomenon of growth is worthy of remark. It commences from a seed deposited in the top of some tree, generally a palm. How it gets placed in such a position is a matter for conjecture, but it is probably through the instrumentality of some bird. Here the seed germinates, but makes all its effort downwards, guided in its descent by the trunk of the tree, which in time it thoroughly encases, and on reaching the earth it immediately takes root. This root, whilst descending, derives sustenance from the tree-trunk, for all the time the seed is putting forth leaves and shoots, from each of which more roots descend earthwards; and so this process continually goes on until the supporting tree is completely destroyed and the banyan stands alone on its own roots, often a hundred or more feet high before coming to the plant proper, from which roots are perpetually descending to earth to form fresh props to the tree, and with each new one more and more ground is taken up.

Proceeding on our way, still rising, we came to what, in very old times, had been a fort, doubtless one of the many that the Tongan invaders erected during their invasion of Upolu in days gone by. It was situated as is usual on a narrow commanding ridge, running down steeply on both sides, the direct path being blocked by both parapet and ditch.

Going still upwards for some time, we came to a halt at an elevation of thirteen hundred and fifty feet above sea-level by aneroid barometer, on the edge of a deep gully, the bottom of which we could not see for the dense bush, though we could plainly hear the river rushing wildly far below.

There was no track, but our way now lay down to the river; so on we went, down an incline which was not far from being perpendicular. However, although rougli on the arms, it was not very difficult work, as the trees were so thick that we could let ourselves down from one to another with comparative ease.

Arrived on a swampy flat, we thrust ourselves with much difficulty through great thickets of bamboo and scrub, and emerged on the river, bounding in sullen, solemn, tumultuous grandeur in sheets of white foam over the black lava rocks.

We were now once more in the valley of the 'Vaisigago,' and, again consulting the aneroid, found that our late descent was five hundred and ten feet.

It was quite a new phase of Samoan scenery. We appeared to be in a rift in the solid rock, which, taking a sudden turn at a short distance both below and above us, left us with but a limited glimpse of the intensely blue sky overhead from our bottom-of-the-well-like position.

Fringing the dark rocks on cither side, the graceful fern-trees, with their drooping fronds almost meeting, formed a fairy avenue of the most lovely description, whilst trees of every shade of foliage, trellised with innumerable gay creepers and hanging mosses, were to be seen, rendering more beautiful still the frequent waterfalls, from ten to thirty feet high, which tumbled down in showers of feathery spray into the shining, shimmering silver pools below, reflecting in their untroubled parts the fathomless azure of the sky above, and passed onwards to the sea with a soothing roar, that found a soft whispering echo in the surrounding cliffs.

Rising sheer on both sides above the cliffs, the ranges stood out boldly, thickly covered with forest. Not a sound was heard but the rushing of the water, which seemed as though it were the natural silence of the place. With this sensation, everything was so quiet and peaceful that, for the moment, one lost all desire to proceed farther on, and wished to remain in this wonderful haven of glorious rest for the remainder of existence.

Stretched at full length on a couch-like rock, with the white water merrily dancing up in front, lazily dreaming and wondering why life should not always be thus, in the fascinating lullaby of the rapidly passing stream I could imagine I heard the sound of old familiar voices far away, and in my mind was answering, when all such fancies were rudely dispelled by the Judge, in whose soul was no poetry, shaking me nearly off my rock, and holding out towards me a frying-pan of gin and water, having brought no cup, inquiring in vulgar, commonplace, earthly language most obnoxious to my then frame of mind, whether I would take a 'tot.'

The 'tot' finished, we picked up our traps and started off again on our course, which now lay directly up the bed of the river, and a most particularly rough track it was. At one moment we were clambering over slippery lava rocks, and jumping from one to the other at the risk of breaking our necks; at another time wading waist-deep in a seething pool of water, while every now and then a waterfall would effectually bar any further direct progress.

When this occurred we took to the steep sides of the gully, cutting our own track with long eighteen-inch bush-knives until we headed the obstacle ; and so the journey proceeded for about two hours, when, arriving at a point where the river became divided, we took to the bush, and, travelling for some little time along a minor ridge, we descended again to the bed of the branch river, after which, crossing and plunging a few yards into the bush, we at last arrived at the 'Fale o le fe'e," the aneroid showing a height of one thousand five hundred feet.

Like very many other sights that one takes so much trouble to get at, this mysterious house did not come up to the expectation we had formed. Our first exclamation on halting at the hallowed spot, which we had endured so much to get at, was, 'Is this all?' We felt as though we had been swindled, and had it not been for the fine healthy exercise we had enjoyed in getting there, and the certain benefit therefrom, with the consequent welcome break in the miserable monotony of Apian existence, I am afraid that we might have used bad language, so disappointed were we.

There was nought to be seen but a few upright stones cropping up through a dense matting of undergrowth which we set to work to clear away. Guided by the upright stones, about six or seven feet high and of irregular thickness, we soon traced out what had been the outer walls of a house of the usual Samoan shape, rounded at both ends. The pillars which were still standing, and others found lying scattered about on the outside boundary, had evidently formed the exterior posts of the house, and bore no traces of dressing, but seemed to have been split from the strata of basaltic rock in the cliffs close by. What means were used in procuring these, either artificial or natural, it is impossible to say; but no doubt fire and water had somewhat to say to it, as the natives at the time the house must have been built had none other than stone tools to work with.

Close by the house stands a lone pillar with a large substantial stone block at its base, upon which it is said that the Fe'e used to sit and overlook his workmen. He probably was some old tyrant chief of former days, but, as tradition relates, his slaves, no longer able to endure his impositions, one day, when they caught him dozing, threw him into the river, in which he was swept down to the reef, and still remains there.

In the centre of the outlined house is a stone rising much higher than the outside ones, and fractured on the top—this most likely was the centre-post; and close to it, evidencing the great antiquity of the ruins, grows a large tree sixty or seventy years old, perhaps more. Nothing is left to show what sort of roof it had, if ever it carried any at all ; and the probability is, if it was covered, that it was not with stone, as amontrst the débris scattered about, no segments of anything approaching an arch-curve are to be found: besides that, there is no indication of sufficient strength of outside wall to sustain the thrust of a stone arch.

It is very likely that there never was any roof at all, but that it was merely a mystic collection of stones similar to our Stonehenge or other Druidical circles. Samoan traditions are very hazy on the subject, merely informing an inquirer that it was built under the management of the devil, but when they don't know; but I heard one very old Samoan say that in times of trouble, or when some important question was to be investigated, the great chiefs would retire there and sit in solemn mystical silence, each one with his back against a stone pillar, until one of them should receive inspiration from the spirits supposed to be hovering round the place, and deliver his instructions in oracular form.

We soon finished our inspection of the ruins, and then went in search of a camping-place; and whilst so doing were anxiously requested not to spit or throw anything into the stream, for if we were to do so, the devil would get enraged and let loose all the upper waters upon us and drown the whole party. Selecting a place high enough above the stream to be comfortably out of the reach of any ordinary diabolical rage in case offence might be given, we set the bearers to construct a house for the night roofed with wild banana-leaves, whilst we bathed and donned comfortable dry clothes.

By this time we were quite ready for feeding, and a fire being started in quick time, the frying-pan, last used as a pannikin at our halting-place by the river, was discoursing rival and more interesting music than that of the bubbling stream, and diffusing around an appetizing odour of fried pork sufficiently attractive to create a soul under the very ribs of death by starvation.

With fingers for forks, sheath-knives for spoons, leaves for plates, biscuit and pork for the sustenance, and tea in a tin billy for drink, we set to work with a will to satisfy the cravings of a trio of most glorious appetites quite unknown in Apia, where one only eats to live, and looks upon meal-times as merely regular events of the day to mark the effluxion of time.

The historical, post-prandial pipe, ever-present in all accounts of camping out that ever were written, with us was conspicuous by its absence, and for the first time in my life I was in the company of three bushmen all non-smokers. Stretched out in our rugs on a banana-leaf carpet, under a roof of the same useful article, a plenteous wood-fire brightly burning at our feet just outside, and illuminating strangely the surrounding trees with its flickering flame, we took our ease and swapped yarns.

Gradually the night closed in, and as gradually did our talking cease, till, lulled by the drowsy murmur of the little river, we dropped off one by one to a well-earned sleep.

On waking up next morning, I was very much disgusted to find that it had rained in the night, with the effect of caving in our roof and filling the house with water. It was scarcely daylight, and the river could be heard absolutely roaring, giving us notice that a freshet had come down suddenly from the heights above, without our having to our knowledge provoked the 'old gentleman;' anyway, it was lucky we had not chosen a lower level for our camp.

Daylight at last broke, and, lighting up the fire, the billy was soon merrily singing out an invitation to tea. Everything had got uncomfortably wet, but it did not much matter, as the temperature was uncommonly mild, and a cup of hot tea and a biscuit and pork soon put things all right.

Going to the river for our morning ablutions, we saw, from traces left, that the stream had at one time during the night risen quite ten feet above its normal level, and was still considerably swollen, affording a plain hint that camping close to such water-courses was by no means safe. After a good bath and breakfast we got on the home-track.

2 O LE FE'E, THE CUTTLE-FISH (OCTOPUS)[2]

GEORGE TURNER

THIS was a war-god said to have been brought by a chief called Tapuaau, who swam hither from Fiji with his cuttle-fish. When taken into a house it showed a special fondness for a piece of white native cloth by stretching over to it, and hence this white cloth became an emblem of the god, and his worshippers in going to battle were known by white turbans, which they thought would please the god and be a defence against the enemy.

Before starting all assembled in the public place of the village, and one of the priests prayed as follows:—

> Le Fe'e e! faafofoga mai ia
> O au o Fale le a tulai atu nei.
> Le Fe'e e! au mai ia ou mūmū fua
> Sei tau a'i le taua nei.

---

[2] Excerpted from George Turner, *Samoa: A Hundred Years Ago and Long Before* (London: Macmillan & Co., 1884)

Which may be translated as follows:—O Fe'e! listen—I am Fale who now stand up—O Fe'e! give us your red flaming rage with which to fight this battle.

All listened carefully to the enunciation of this prayer by the priest, for if he was observed to *stutter* in a single word it was a bad omen.

The Fe'e was also supposed to be present in the white shell of the *Cyprœa ovula*; hence a string of these shells was suspended in the house of the priest, and were supposed to murmur, or "cry," when war was determined on. The colour of the shells was also watched. A clear white was a good omen, but if they looked dark and dingy it was a bad one.

The movements of the cuttle-fish at sea were also looked after at war-times. If seen near the shore when the people were mustering for battle it was a good sign; if far off the reverse.

I N one place the Fe'e was a general village god, whose province was not confined to war. The month of May was sacred to his worship. No traveller was then allowed to pass through the village by the public road; nor was any canoe allowed in the lagoon off that part of the settlement. There was great feasting, too, on these occasions, and also games, club exercise, spear-throwing, wrestling, etc.

A new temple was at this time erected, to the material of which every man, woman, and child contributed something, even if only a stick or a reed of thatch. Some were drafted off to put up the house, and the rest commenced to fight in real earnest, and settle any old grudges with each other. He who got the most wounds was set down for special favours from the god. With the completion of the temple the fighting ended, and that was to suffice for the year. A quarrel of neighbours at any other time, and rising to blows, was frowned upon by the god Fe'e, because it was not left till next year and temple-building day.

In another district three months were sacred to the worship of the Fe'e. During that time any one passing along the road, or in the lagoon, would be beaten, if not killed, for insulting the god. For the first month torches and all other lights were forbidden, as the god was about and did not wish to be seen. White turbans were also forbidden during the festivities, and confined to war. At this time, also, all unsightly projecting burdens—such as a log of firewood on the shoulder—were forbidden, lest it should be considered by the god as a mockery of his *tentacula*.

The priest at this place had a large wooden bowl, which he called lipi, or *sudden death*. This was another representative of the god, and by this the family had no small gains. In a case of stealing, fine mats or other gifts were taken by the injured party to the priest to curse the thief and make him ill. The priest would then sit down with some select members of the family around the bowl representative of the god, and pray for speedy vengeance on the guilty; then they waited the issue. These imprecations were dreaded. Conscience-stricken thieves, when taken ill, were carried off by their friends on a litter and laid down at the door of the priest, with taro, cocoa-nuts, or yams, in lieu of those confessed to have been stolen; and they would add fine mats and other presents, that the priest might pray again over the death-bowl, and have the sentence reversed.

There is a story that the cuttle-fish gods of Savaii were once chased by an Upolu hero, who caught them in a great net and killed them. They were changed into stones, and now stand up in a rocky part of the lagoon on the north side of Upolu. For a long time travelling parties from Savaii felt *eerie* when they came to the place—did not like to go through between the stones, but took the outside passage.

Another fragment makes out that a Savaii Fe'e married the daughter of a chief on Upolu, and for convenience in coming and going made a hole in the reef, and hence the harbour at Apia. He went up the river also at that place, and built a stone house inland, the "Stonehenge" relics of which are still pointed out, and named to this day "the house of the Fe'e." In time of war he sent a branch drifting down the river as a good omen, and a sign to the people that they might go on with the war, sure of driving the enemy.

IN some instances the Fe'e was a household god only. If any visitor caught a cuttle-fish and cooked it, or if any member of that family had been where a cuttle-fish was eaten, the family would meet over the case, and a man or woman would be selected to go and lie down in a *cold* oven, and be covered over with leaves, as in the process of baking, and all this as a would-be or mock burnt-offering to avert the wrath of the god. While this was being done the family united in praying: "O bald-headed Fe'e! forgive what has been done —it was all the work of a *stranger*." Failing such signs of respect and humility, it was supposed the god would come to the family, and cause a cuttle-fish to grow internally, and be the death of some of them.

3 "O LE FALE-O-LE-FE'E": OR, RUINS OF AN OLD SAMOAN TEMPLE[3]

JOHN B. STAIR

THE priesthood of Samoa were of different classes and of varied influence, so that, although having no idols or idol-worship in later generations as in other groups, their influence was great and widely felt. The Tahitians were accustomed to scoff at this absence of idolatory, and call them the "Godless Samoans"; but, they were happily free from the tyranny of human sacrifices, and, to some degree, also of the lascivious worship that prevailed amongst the Tahitians, and devastated many other fair and beautiful groups. Still, for all that, the religious system of the Samoans was extensive and galling in its oppressiveness; "Lords many, and Gods many," abounding and crushing the people with their exactions and superstitious fears. *Aitus,* or spirits, of varied dispositions and power, were numerous, filling the people with alarm and dread.

---

[3] John B. Stair, "'*O Le Fala-O-Le-Fe'e*': Or, Ruins of an Old Samoan Temple," *Journal of the Polynesian Society* 3, no. 3 (1894).

The priesthood, *Taula-aitu,* or "Anchors of the spirits" (from *Inula,* an anchor, and *Aitu,* a spirit), may be subdivided into four classes, viz.: Priests of the war-gods, Keepers of the wargods, Family Priests, and Prophets or Sorcerers. Of these, the *Taula-aitu,* or "Anchors of the Spirits," had great influence, and were consulted upon all warlike questions. They invoked the assistance of the various war-gods, of whom the most celebrated was *Nafanua,* a female deity reverenced by the whole people; and who, in conjunction with *Savea-sio-leo,* may be looked upon as the national gods of war of Samoa. In addition to these, however, each separate district had its own special war-god or gods. As for instance:

Name of god	Reverenced by.
O le Tamafainga	"Manono" and "O le faasaleleanga."
O Tui-o-Pulotu	"Fangaloa," and part of "Upolu."
O Turitau	"Falealili."
O Tui-leo-nu'nu	"A'ana," and "O le Tnamasanga."
O le Fe'e	"A'ana," and Faleata.
Aitu-i-Pava	"Le Faasale laenga."
Tui Fiti	"Matautu," and "Gaga'eole-moonga."
Nafanua	"Oagaifo-o-le-mounga."
Sepomalosi, Moso, and Tui Atua	"Leone," and " Pangopango."

It was one of this class, *Taulaaitu,* the representative of the war-god of *Manono, O le Tamafainga,* that usurped the regal power of the islands, on the death of the last king of his line, *Safe-o-fafine*; and, who reigned until his tyranny became unbearable, when he was killed by the people of *A'ana,* in 1829.

The *Taiui-aitu-tau* (keepers of the war-gods), (or, as they were further called, *Vaa-faatau-o-aitu-tau* warships of the war-gods), had also very great influence. To their custody were committed the objects supposed to be inhabited by the district war-gods. These emblems, or symbols were various, and had different names. The fleets of Manono were accompanied by two of such, *Limulimuta* and and *Samalulu*; the former a kind of drum, and the latter a pennant or streamer, which floated from the masthead of the sacred canoe. In the district of *O le Tuamasanga* the emblems consisted of the *pu*, or conch shell, called, *O Aitulangi* (gods of the heavens). The same symbol was used by the warriors of *Matautu*, on *Savaii*, whilst at *Bangaloa*, in *Atua*, the symbol of the god's presence was a large box, or chest, placed upon the canoe of the priest of the war-god, and accompanied the fleet into battle. Another significant emblem used by the warriors of the latter place resembled a broom, or besom, which was carried, like the broom of Van Tromp, at the masthead of the war-priest's canoe. The *pu*, or conch shell, was always carried by the keeper of the war-god on land, when the *Tuamatanga*, or *Matautu*, were engaged in battle; but the other emblems were only taken in the canoes.

The *Faleaitu*, or spirit-houses, were objects of great reverence. Some *aitus*, mostly the war-gods, if not entirely so, were honored with them. These spirit-houses were also called *O le Malumalu o le aitu* (the Temple of the god), one of which, of more or less dignity, was usually found in every settlement.

They were generally built in the common circular or elliptical shape, and, although there might be nothing in their finish or build to distinguish them from other houses, they were always regarded with reverence, and even with dread; so that, for a long time after the arrival of the Europeans, the natives were accustomed to resent any intrusion upon their sacred precincts. These temples, or spirit-houses, were always in charge of the keepers of the war-gods, who, in addition to their other titles, were called *Vaa Taua* (war-ships). The emblems of the god were always placed in these temples, and given into the care of the keepers.

When the *Taula aitu* (priests of the gods) were consulted professionally, they were accustomed to visit these temples for the purpose of advising with the god, who was supposed to enter into the symbol or emblem of the deity and then deliver their answers to the questions asked. The spirit-houses were usually placed in the principal *Marae* of the village, and were built of similar materials to those of ordinary dwellings. They were usually built upon raised platforms of stone *(fanua tanu),* varying in height and dimensions according to the respect felt towards the god by the builders. These stone platforms were made, and the houses built, by the united labour of those interested, whether of a family, or village, or district.

One interesting exception to the usual style of building these spirit-houses came under my notice shortly before leaving the islands, in 1845.

O le Fale o le Fe'e (the Temple of the fe'e), the war-god of A'ana, Upolu, was formerly a place of great renown and importance, but of late years its glory has departed. Its history was described to me in such a way, that I determined to visit it and see for myself the marvels described. Not only were there the remains of the temple of the god, but quantities of coral that he had carried up from the reef into the mountains lay scattered on every side. I found that comparatively few had actually visited the spot, but the name of the place was familiar as also the wonderful stories of the famous fale ma'a, or stone house of the god. The large blocks of coral, requiring several men to lift them, were scattered about the temple, and which the god had carried up from the reef single-handed.

At last, meeting a man who seemed to have a good knowledge of the place, I arranged to visit it. My friend, J. O. Williams, Esq., the British Consul at Apia, volunteered to accompany me, several influential natives from my own district, and also of Apia, gladly going with us. We started from Apia in good time, full of eager curiosity. Several miles inland we reached a point of interest, as the track led directly through the great fortress or Olo, of O le Vaemaunga, deserted at that time, but which had played an important part in many a struggle of the past. We found the Olo of considerable extent, and protected by the steep sides of a precipice or deep ditch, and an embankment of earth. In time of war, the gap through which the road passed was closed by a strong stockade, and defended by a large body of troops.

As we neared the spot of our search the footpath wound down the steep sides of a precipitous mountain into a valley, the bottom of which formed the bed of a mountain torrent, which, fortunately for our excursion, was dry at the time of our visit. Crossing this valley, a short distance brought us to another river-bed, down which a small stream was quietly threading its way among the smoothly worn blocks of lava scattered over the torrent bed. We followed its upward course for some little time, when our guide suddenly sprang upon the bank, and glancing around the spot near which he stood, hastily exclaimed, "*O lenei le fale, o le Fe'e* (here is the house of the *Fe'e)*. We followed, curious as to what would meet our view. My first impressions were those of disappointment, since little could be seen but the thick growth of brushwood and forest trees which covered the spot; but these feelings soon gave place to others of a more pleasing character. Our guide commenced in good earnest to clear away the brush-wood and undergrowth that covered the place, and as we all joined in the work the ground was soon cleared, and the remains of the far-famed *Fale-o-le-Fe'e,* or house of the *Fe'e* were laid bare before us.

We soon discovered that the house had been built of the usual round or elliptical shape, but that the builders, whoever they were, had substituted slabs of basalt for the wooden posts usually placed to support the eaves, as is the case almost universally with the Samoans; so much so, that I believe this is the only known instance of a departure from this rule. Whatever had been the character of the roof formally used, it had long since perished, and the centre slab of stone that supported it had fallen, whilst the place of the roof itself was supplied by two large forest trees which covered the ruins, and whose far-reaching and strongly buttressed roots were spread out over the site of the floor of the house.

"We found twelve or thirteen of the smaller stone posts still standing, but the large centre slabs lay broken in the middle of the circle. The outer posts, which were still standing, were about four feet out of the ground, whilst the centre slabs appear to have been originally about twelve or thirteen feet in length, fifteen or eighteen inches in width, and seven or eight inches thick. The ends had been inserted in the ground, and I imagine that, when placed upright, another slab had been laid horizontally upon them, from which other slabs or posts were raised to support the roof. Several of our party had seen these centre slabs standing not long before, and could thus testify to their appearance. It was said that lately some young fellows, hunting wild pigs, had passed the spot, and amused themselves by pelting the slabs arid throwing them down.

Fortunately they left another interesting relic of the olden times intact. At about six or eight feet on the left-hand-side of the ruins was a small stone platform, or seat, still remaining, and which was perfect. Whether it had been used as a seat for the priest, or altar, was hard to say; but from the sloping stone support at the back, I fancy it had been used as a seat by the priest. I have also thought it may have been used as a coronation seat, or post of honor, at the inauguration ceremonies of a chiefs installation.

The house had been forty-eight feet in length by forty-five in breadth. One portion of the floor of the house had been covered with a pavement of neatly placed slabs of stone; but these had begun to be displaced. As I looked upon this relic of bygone ages, many questions arose; foremost of which came the thought, from whence had these huge slabs of stone been obtained, and how had they been wrought by the natives, with their absence of tools, into there present shape? The former question was soon answered, for close at hand were masses of the same kind of basaltic rock exposed from the side of a precipice, and from which large quantities had evidently been quarried. I might have been puzzled to answer the other question as to how the slabs had been wrought, had I not known that the Samoans adopted a very simple but ingenious plan to split and rend similar stones. That particular kind of basalt, especially, splits easily, and a heavy blow soon rends a detached block; but when the natives require to split the solid bed rock, they clear off the mould that may be on the surface, kindle a fire upon it in the direction in which they wish the fracture to run, and then, when the stone is sufficiently heated, they dash cold water over the heated surface, and their work, so far as rending the rock is concerned, is accomplished. I looked with interest upon these relics of the past, and longed to know more of their history than it was possible to obtain. I made a rough sketch of the old seat and remains of the house, the natives looking on the while, and apparently wondering what there could be in the scene to so deeply interest me. Another question would naturally arise, as to how such huge masses of stone could be moved such distances as they sometimes were. In the present case the distance was not great, but the blocks were too heavy to be lifted, in many cases. I think there can be no doubt they were always shifted, or dragged, on rollers or small skids; removed and re-laid as needed—an old world method of removing heavy burdens that was found in common use in this distant portion of its boundaries.

After we had satisfied our curiosity at the old ruin, our guides, anxious to make good the whole of their statements, drew my attention to the so-called coral, said to be found in the bed of the torrent, and which formed one great marvel of the story. It was said to be of three different kinds, and all brought from the reef. It was in vain we told them it was not coral at all, but a substance formed in the neighbouring stream. They laughed at our statement; but could scarcely believe their eyes when I split one of the blocks of the so-called coral in half and showed them various leaves and small twigs embedded in it, asking them at the same time if they had ever seen such coral as that on the reef. That revelation seemed to confound them, but they still stoutly contended for the old story.

From thence they led us up the bed of the stream to show us what they called the larger blocks of coral, but which proved to be calcareous spar of a more compact formation. Failing to convince us here, they conducted us to the spot where the *amu,* or branch-coral was to be found; but, on getting there, we were disappointed to find that a portion of the rock had fallen down since our principal guide was last there, and filled the place where the *amu,* or branch-coral, had formally been found. This place had been a large natural basin at the foot of a precipice, into which the stream fell from above, forming a small cascade, and in which these calcareous formations had evidently been deposited. These latter pieces had certainly very much the appearance of real branch-coral, so that I did not wonder at the general and long sustained delusion; but the faith of our native companions seemed utterly staggered upon our finding some of the so-called coral, or, as they proved to be, stalactites, actually forming upon the surface of a portion of the rock, similar to the substance which had been for so long a time mistaken for coral. It seemed hard to destroy such a long-cherished delusion, but so it was to be, and from that time forth the doings of the *Aitu* seemed to be sadly at a discount.

The little that we could gather about this old ruin was this:—The god, or *Aitu,* in the form of a cuttle-fish (o *le Fe'e)* was stated to have been brought from Savaii, by a woman, to

Apia; but, on reaching that place he made his escape from the basket in which he was carried, and following the course of the mountain torrent bed, he had reached this spot, far inland, where he took up his abode, and in process of time made the place famous. He certainly had selected a romantic spot, and there was much connected with it to awe the mind of the beholder when under the influence of dread. Even as we looked upon the surroundings, there was much to arrest attention. The high mountains on either side of the valley; the mountain torrent, and frowning precipice, combined with the solemn grandeur and stillness of the place, all seemed to mark it as a fitting residence for such a mysterious personage; and, as a consequence, a strong feeling of sacredness and mystery had long been attached to the spot.

A Samoan Chief's Mountain Burial Place.

ON the summit of one of the neighbouring mountain tops the burial place of some chiefs of high rank *of O le Vae maunga* district was pointed out to me by my guide, as an object of interest, where for many ages the heads of various chiefs had been interred, to save them from molestation and insult in time of war. I listened with great interest to his description; but, it was getting late, and we had a long journey before us to the coast, so that I was obliged to defer my visit to the spot until another opportunity, a purpose which I was unfortunately unable to carry out.

At length, and after a lapse of some fifty years, the circumstance is again brought to my recollection in a peculiar manner. During the last few months an old friend, and one of the very few old Samoan Missionaries now left, the Rev. S. Ella, of Sydney, but formerly of Samoa, brought under my notice a paper that he had read before the Ethnological section of the Australasian Association for the Advancement of Science, at their Adelaide meeting, in which he alluded to some remarks of the late Mr. Handley Sterndale, respecting some remarkable stone remains he had discovered, many years since, whilst rambling in the interior of the island of Upolu, Samoa, which are described in the first number of the Journal of the Polynesian Society.

Speaking of Mr. Sterndale's discovery, Mr. Ella says:— "Whilst rambling in the interior of the island, he came to a lofty spur of a mountain, with a volcanic centre. He crossed several deep ravines down which flowed mountain torrents. One of these ravines had been converted by the hand of man into a fosse. In some parts it was excavated; in others, built up at the sides with large stones; and, in one place he found a parapet wall. He climbed up this gully, and passed through a narrow opening in the wall unto a level space before him, where he made the discoveries he spoke of."

Amongst other remarkable stone relics he found, "a conical structure of huge dimensions, about 20ft. high and 100ft. in diameter, built of large basalt blocks, some of which he considered to have been above a ton weight, which were laid in even courses. In two places near the top he marked what appeared to have been entrances to the interior. He entered a low cave or vault, choked with rock and roots of trees. He found appearances of narrow chambers within. Mr. Sterndale thought that the pyramidal structure at one time formed the foundation of some building of importance. Many other foundations of 10ft. high were near it. He also observed a number of stone cairns, apparently graves, disposed in rows."

I feel quite satisfied that these small cairns, of which Mr. Sterndale speaks, were, as he supposed, graves, in which were buried the heads of various chiefs interred, after the custom so common to the Samoans, and that this spot which he visited on that occasion was the burial place pointed out to me, or one similar to it. And, further, on reading his description of the country he passed over before reaching it, I think he must have traversed the route by which we journeyed. Our descriptions, though written so widely apart, seem to tally. It also seems probable that the masses of rock he describes as forming the great structure he alludes to, were procured from the same precipice, or quarry, of which I have spoken.

4 THE OCTOPUS GOD OF WAR IN SAMOAN MYTHOLOGY[4]

JOHN B. STAIR

A s every settlement has its local god of war in addition to the national war-gods, so every family has its own particular *aitu,* or tutelary deity, who was usually considered to inhabit some familiar object. One family supposed their god to possess a shark; another, some bird or a stone; and another, a reptile. Thus a great variety of objects, animate and inanimate, were reverenced by the Samoans. Their feelings with respect to these guardian deities do not appear to have been very sensitive, as although the members of one family were accustomed to regard a given object, say a shark, with superstitious reverence as their family god, they were continually seeing the same fish killed and eaten by others around them. In the case of local or district war-gods the entire district were careful to protect their chosen object of reverence from insult. Still, it often happened that if the

---

[4] Excerpted from John B. Stair, *Old Samoa; or, Flotsam and Jetsam from the Pacific Ocean* (Religious Tract Society, 1897).

gods were not propitious to their suppliants, torrents of abuse were heaped upon them; but, as a rule, the chosen deities were much dreaded. Many of these gods were supposed to dwell in the Făfā, or else in Sā-le-Fe'e, whilst others ruled in Pulotu.

O le Făfā, Sā-le-Fe'e, and Pulotu are places which occupy a prominent position in Samoan mythology, and seem in some manner to be connected the one with the other.

O le Făfā (Hades) is alike the entrance to Sā-le-Fe'e, the Samoan Tartarus, or dread place of punishment, and also to Pulotu, the abode of the blest; the one entrance being called *O le Lua-loto-o-Alii,* or deep hole of chiefs, by which they passed to Pulotu; the other, *O le Lualoto-o-tau-fanua,* or deep hole of the common people, by which they passed to *Le nu'u-o-nonoa,* or the land of the bound, which is simply another term for the muchdreaded Sa-le-Fe'e. The idea of the superiority of the chiefs over the common people was thus perpetuated, none but chiefs or higher ranks gaining entrance to the Samoan Elysium.

Speaking of the condition of the dead, an old chief of Savaii once told me that there were supposed to be two places to which they went, the one called *O le nulu-o-Aitu,* or land of spirits; the other, *O le nu'u-o-nonoa,* the land of the bound; their bondage being superintended by such vindictive spirits as Moso, Ita-nga-tā, and other deities who hold sway there, whilst the significant name itself is, I think, simply another name for Sā-le-Fe'e.

It is interesting to notice how much this name O le Fe'e is mixed up with Samoan mythology, whether as the name of a renowned war-god and deity, or as Sā-le-Fe'e, the much-dreaded regions below; as also with a mysterious building of the distant past known as *O le faleo-le-Fe'e,* the house of the *Fe'e,* the ruins of which still remain as mute witnesses of a by-gone worship of which the Samoans now have no knowledge or record whatever, save the name. All these facts point to it as a name of deep significance and meaning in the history of the past, whether in connexion with the history of the ancestors of the present race of Samoans or, as many think, with the records of an earlier, but long since extinct, race. A halo of mystery and romance seems thrown around the name which has been selected as the name of the war-god of A'ana, *O le Fe'e* (octopus). At some future time light may be thrown upon the subject, but at present all seems mysterious.

The disembodied spirit was supposed to retain the exact resemblance of its former self, and immediately on leaving the body it was believed to commence its solitary journey to the Fafa, which was located to the westward of Savaii, the most westerly of the group, and towards this point disembodied spirits from all the islands bent their way immediately after death. Thus in case of a spirit commencing its journey at Manu'a, the most easterly of the group, it journeyed on to the western end of that island from whence it started, where it dived into the sea and swam to the nearest point of Tutuila, where, having journeyed along the shore to the extreme west point of that island, it again plunged into the sea and pursued its solitary way to the next island, and thus onward throughout the entire group until it reached the extreme west point of Savaii, the most westerly island, where it finally dived into the ocean and pursued its solitary way to the mysterious Fāfā. At the west point of Upolu the land terminates in a narrow rocky point, which is still known as *O le fatu-osofia* (the leaping-stone), from which all spirits were said to leap into the sea *en route* to the Fāfā. This was a much-dreaded point, where the lonely travellers were said to be certainly met with, and their company was anything but desired. I well remember the astonishment expressed at the daring courage of a man I well knew who, after he became a Christian, built his house upon this haunted point.

    *   *   *   *   *   *   *   *   *

ALL the different orders of the priesthood possessed great influence over the minds of the people, who were kept in constant fear by their threats, and impoverished by their exactions. This remark applies more particularly to the two latter classes, although frequent offerings were made by the people to their war-gods, with which the priests, or *Taulā-aitu,* failed not to enrich themselves. There would seem to have been a strong resemblance between this class of priests and the Maori *tohunga,* with their much-dreaded incantations.

Some *aitu,* principally the war-gods, but not entirely so, were honoured with dwellings called *Fale-aitu* (spirithouses), as also *O le Mālumālu-o-le-aitu* (the dwelling or temple of the *aitu),* whether a house or a tree, one or more of which of some description were usually found in every village. These spirit-houses were built in the usual shape and style, with nothing in their build or finish to distinguish them from other dwellings, being at times mere huts, but rendered sacred by their being set apart as the dwelling-place of the god, and hence regarded with much veneration by the Samoans in the olden times; so much so that for a considerable period after the arrival of Europeans amongst them, they were accustomed to view with much jealousy any intrusion upon their sacred precincts. They were placed in charge of the keepers of the war-gods, who, in addition to their titles given elsewhere, were also called *Va'a-fa'atan-o-aitu-tau* (war-ships of the war-gods). Whatever emblems of deity were in possession of the village were always placed in these houses, and under the watchful care of these keepers.

When the priests of the war-gods were consulted professionally, they were accustomed to go to these houses for the purpose of advising with the god, who was supposed to enter into the priest, as well as the particular emblems of the deity, in case any were deposited in the temple, and then deliver his answer to the proposed question.

These spirit-houses, or *Mālumālu-o-le-aitu,* were usually placed in the principal *malae* of the village, surrounded with a low fence, and were built of similar materials to those used in ordinary dwellings. They were almost always placed on *fanua-tanu*, or raised platforms of stones, varying in height and dimensions, according to the amount of respect felt towards the presiding god of the temple by those who erected them. These platforms were always made, and the *Malumalu*, or spirit-house, built, by the united exertions of a whole family, village, or district, as the case may be.

SAMOAN TEMPLES

One very interesting exception to the usual style of building these temples is found in the case of a remarkable old ruin of the *Fale-o-le-Fe'e* (house of the *Fe'e)*, the famous war-god of A'ana and Faleata, the site of which became known to me a short time before leaving Samoa in 1845. This appears to have been built in the usual Samoan style, but its ruins disclose the fact that its builders had used stone slabs for the supporting-posts of the roof, and thus it got the name of *O le fale-ma'ao-le-Fe'e* (the stone house of the *Fe'e)*, and hence became enshrouded with much mystery and wonder. I think this is the only instance of such a departure from the usual style of Samoan building known in the islands.

5 THE OCTOPUS GOD IN TONGA [5]

E. E. V. COLLOCOT

HAELE-FEKE, literally "the Octopus comes," or "Coming in the Octopus," is a god which appeared in the octopus (*feke*). He is also called Tutula, already mentioned as the companion of Faimalie and Faka-fumaka in their journey to Bulotu. Haele-feke is the god of Motua-buaka (lit. Old Pig), an important *matabule* of the Tui Kanokupolu, and of Kioa, the head of a younger branch of the same clan. The clans of Motua-buaka and Kioa, inhabiting a cluster of villa-ges in the western district of Tongatabu, refrained from eating the small octopus which is a favourite delicacy of the majority of Tongans.

The octopus god used to appear ashore in a pool called Kanakana. It is said that he changed into a lizard when travelling overland. When an octopus appeared in this pool it was at once recognised as the god, and the priestess immediately

[5] Excerpted from E. E. V. Collocot, "Notes on Tongan Religion, Part II," *Journal of the Polynesian Society* 30 (1921).

went and awaited him at the shrine, apparently a little raised platform, whither presently the people resorted with bunches of coconuts and plaited coconut leaves and earth. The priestess spoke as the octopus, and from words used by an informant would seem to have imitated an octopus, presumably sprawling out in the manner of this ungainly creature.

The people of this deity not only eschewed in their own diet the flesh of the octopus, but they must not approach a place where he was being eaten. If any transgressed the *tabu* he was afflicted with complete baldness, which, however, could be cured by suitable supplications. Should any of the octopus people find one of their gods dead they gave him decent and ceremonious burial in Teekiu, their head village. With this god was connected the large cowrie shell (*bule*), from whose movements auguries were read. The connection perhaps arises from the use of the shell in octopus-fishing, or both facts have a common origin. A cowrie-shell forms the centre of the bait, which is furnished with artificial tentacles, and somewhat resembles an octopus. This on being lowered into the water is clasped by the octopus, who is then hauled up and taken.

OCTOPUS (LEFT) IN STONE "HOUSE" (CAVE) WITH SQUID

3765893R00028

Printed in Great Britain
by Amazon.co.uk, Ltd.,
Marston Gate.